G000091399

THE ROYAL
HORTICULTURAL
SOCIETY

DIARY
2021

First published in 2020 by Frances Lincoln Publishing,
an imprint of The Quarto Group.
The Old Brewery, 6 Blundell Street
London, N7 9BH
United Kingdom
T (0)20 7700 6700
www.QuartoKnows.com

A catalogue record for this book is available
from the British Library.

ISBN 978 0 7112 4731 4

10 9 8 7 6 5 4 3 2 1

Design by Sarah Pyke

Printed in China

Title page *Iris douglasiana*. This painting is one
of a collection of paintings owned by the British
Iris Society

Below Yellow Crown Imperial. *(Fritillaria)*;
watercolour on paper

RHS FLOWER SHOWS 2021
The Royal Horticultural Society holds a number of
prestigious flower shows throughout the year. At
the time of going to press, show dates for 2021 had
not been confirmed but details can be found on the
website at: rhs.org.uk/shows-events

Every effort is made to ensure calendarial data is
correct at the time of going to press but the publisher
cannot accept any liability for any errors or changes.

CALENDAR 2021

JANUARY
M	T	W	T	F	S	S
				1	2	3
4	5	6	7	8	9	10
11	12	13	14	15	16	17
18	19	20	21	22	23	24
25	26	27	28	29	30	31

FEBRUARY
M	T	W	T	F	S	S
1	2	3	4	5	6	7
8	9	10	11	12	13	14
15	16	17	18	19	20	21
22	23	24	25	26	27	28

MARCH
M	T	W	T	F	S	S
1	2	3	4	5	6	7
8	9	10	11	12	13	14
15	16	17	18	19	20	21
22	23	24	25	26	27	28
29	30	31				

APRIL
M	T	W	T	F	S	S
			1	2	3	4
5	6	7	8	9	10	11
12	13	14	15	16	17	18
19	20	21	22	23	24	25
26	27	28	29	30		

MAY
M	T	W	T	F	S	S
					1	2
3	4	5	6	7	8	9
10	11	12	13	14	15	16
17	18	19	20	21	22	23
24	25	26	27	28	29	30
31						

JUNE
M	T	W	T	F	S	S
	1	2	3	4	5	6
7	8	9	10	11	12	13
14	15	16	17	18	19	20
21	22	23	24	25	26	27
28	29	30				

JULY
M	T	W	T	F	S	S
			1	2	3	4
5	6	7	8	9	10	11
12	13	14	15	16	17	18
19	20	21	22	23	24	25
26	27	28	29	30	31	

AUGUST
M	T	W	T	F	S	S
						1
2	3	4	5	6	7	8
9	10	11	12	13	14	15
16	17	18	19	20	21	22
23	24	25	26	27	28	29
30	31					

SEPTEMBER
M	T	W	T	F	S	S
		1	2	3	4	5
6	7	8	9	10	11	12
13	14	15	16	17	18	19
20	21	22	23	24	25	26
27	28	29	30			

OCTOBER
M	T	W	T	F	S	S
				1	2	3
4	5	6	7	8	9	10
11	12	13	14	15	16	17
18	19	20	21	22	23	24
25	26	27	28	29	30	31

NOVEMBER
M	T	W	T	F	S	S
1	2	3	4	5	6	7
8	9	10	11	12	13	14
15	16	17	18	19	20	21
22	23	24	25	26	27	28
29	30					

DECEMBER
M	T	W	T	F	S	S
		1	2	3	4	5
6	7	8	9	10	11	12
13	14	15	16	17	18	19
20	21	22	23	24	25	26
27	28	29	30	31		

CALENDAR 2022

JANUARY
M	T	W	T	F	S	S
					1	2
3	4	5	6	7	8	9
10	11	12	13	14	15	16
17	18	19	20	21	22	23
24	25	26	27	28	29	30
31						

FEBRUARY
M	T	W	T	F	S	S
	1	2	3	4	5	6
7	8	9	10	11	12	13
14	15	16	17	18	19	20
21	22	23	24	25	26	27
28						

MARCH
M	T	W	T	F	S	S
	1	2	3	4	5	6
7	8	9	10	11	12	13
14	15	16	17	18	19	20
21	22	23	24	25	26	27
28	29	30	31			

APRIL
M	T	W	T	F	S	S
				1	2	3
4	5	6	7	8	9	10
11	12	13	14	15	16	17
18	19	20	21	22	23	24
25	26	27	28	29	30	

MAY
M	T	W	T	F	S	S
						1
2	3	4	5	6	7	8
9	10	11	12	13	14	15
16	17	18	19	20	21	22
23	24	25	26	27	28	29
30	31					

JUNE
M	T	W	T	F	S	S
		1	2	3	4	5
6	7	8	9	10	11	12
13	14	15	16	17	18	19
20	21	22	23	24	25	26
27	28	29	30			

JULY
M	T	W	T	F	S	S
				1	2	3
4	5	6	7	8	9	10
11	12	13	14	15	16	17
18	19	20	21	22	23	24
25	26	27	28	29	30	31

AUGUST
M	T	W	T	F	S	S
1	2	3	4	5	6	7
8	9	10	11	12	13	14
15	16	17	18	19	20	21
22	23	24	25	26	27	28
29	30	31				

SEPTEMBER
M	T	W	T	F	S	S
			1	2	3	4
5	6	7	8	9	10	11
12	13	14	15	16	17	18
19	20	21	22	23	24	25
26	27	28	29	30		

OCTOBER
M	T	W	T	F	S	S
					1	2
3	4	5	6	7	8	9
10	11	12	13	14	15	16
17	18	19	20	21	22	23
24	25	26	27	28	29	30
31						

NOVEMBER
M	T	W	T	F	S	S
	1	2	3	4	5	6
7	8	9	10	11	12	13
14	15	16	17	18	19	20
21	22	23	24	25	26	27
28	29	30				

DECEMBER
M	T	W	T	F	S	S
			1	2	3	4
5	6	7	8	9	10	11
12	13	14	15	16	17	18
19	20	21	22	23	24	25
26	27	28	29	30	31	

Rear Admiral John Paul Wellington Furse
(1904–1978) CB, OBE, VMH.

The illustrations featured in these pages offer a tantalising insight into the wide range and variety of bulbous plants that were recorded and collected by John Paul Wellington Furse, from expeditions he undertook to the Near and Middle East between 1960–1976.

John Paul Wellington Furse, or Paul Furse as he was more commonly known, was born on 13 October 1904 in Surrey, England. Son of Dame Katharine Furse, Director of the Women's Royal Naval Service during WWI, and Charles Furse, a successful portrait artist, Paul Furse entered the Navy's engineering college at the age of 13, following which he became a sub-mariner. He served during the Second World War, rising to the position of Rear Admiral prior to his retirement in 1959. Botanising and painting clearly ran in the family. Marianne North, the Victorian plant explorer and painter, was his mother's aunt. Furse spent time with his grandmother in the Alps as a child where he developed an appreciation for alpine plants as well as learning to paint and draw. His interest in plants and illustration continued throughout his naval career.

Following his retirement, Paul Furse undertook several expeditions to the Near and Middle East, accompanied by his wife Polly. Furse had a passion for and specialist knowledge of fritillarias, but irises, daffodils, tulips, crocus, colchicums, lilies and many more bulbous plants feature heavily in his collecting notes and illustrations. In fact, it has been suggested that Furse drew nearly every known species of lily during his lifetime. The first plant collecting trip took place in 1960. Furse drove with Polly from England, to the mountains of north-eastern Turkey and Iran. According to Kit Strange, this area had been chosen deliberately as it had been little explored since the nineteenth century.[1]

A Land Rover packed full of equipment enabled them to access some of the challenging mountain passes. Amongst those in the party was Patrick Synge, then Editor of the Journal of the Royal Horticultural Society, who recorded that they covered just over 6,000 miles whilst in Turkey and Persia, during an intensive period of two months.[2] Over the course of the next sixteen years, the plant collecting trips undertaken by Paul Furse were to have a significant impact: '[these trips] resulted in the most extensive collection of choice bulbs from Afghanistan, Iran and Turkey at Wisley that has ever been accumulated. Many of the bulbs had to be collected blind out of flower, so that in the next spring season Paul and Polly would drive over to Wisley and he would paint and record each one as it flowered. So each form and variant was recorded in a mass of drawings, [photographs] and notes on which future students can draw since he gave most of them to the library of the RHS.'[3]

There are over 800 watercolours by Furse in the Lindley Art Collections, collecting notes and letters are held in the RHS Wisley herbarium and the living plant specimens were also held at Wisley. Dried specimens were deposited in the herbarium at RBG Kew, in excess of 700 illustrations are held in the library there and 25 boxes of correspondence field notes and collecting notes reside in the archives. The illustrations in the Lindley Library are signed and dated, with complete botanical names or a close approximation. A personal system of 'PF' reference numbers allows the illustrations to be cross-checked against the collecting notes, and detailed locations reveal not just the place name, but soil type, vegetation, associated plants and altitude at which a specimen was found.

When not travelling, Furse was also heavily involved with activities at the RHS. He was Vice-Chairman of the Lily Group and he also produced numerous books and botanical articles. Furse first exhibited paintings at RHS shows in the 1930s, he continued to exhibit and was awarded four RHS Gold medals for his paintings between 1964 and 1968. In 1965 he was awarded the RHS Victoria Medal of Honour, in recognition of his contribution as a plant collector. Furse left a legacy of records that both researchers and students can consult. Synge observed that Paul and Polly 'advised, encouraged and helped other travellers to the area in any way they could.'[4]

Charlotte Brooks, Art Curator, RHS Lindley Library

With grateful thanks to Martyn Rix for his contribution to the text and Vikky Furse for permission to reproduce the illustrations.

1. Kit Strange, 'Paul Furse and his plant collections at Kew', Curtis's Botanical Magazine, 2007 (1)
2. JRHS, Vol. 86 (1961) pp. 256-270: 'A Plant-Collecting Expedition to the Mountains of North-Eastern Turkey and Northern Iran' by Patrick M. Synge
3. Obituary: 'Paul Furse' by Patrick Synge RHS Lilies (1978/9) pp.88-89
4. Bulletin of the Alpine Garden Society, Vol. 45 (1977) pp. 112-119: 'Paul Furse and His Paintings' by P.M. Synge

28 Monday

29 Tuesday

30 Wednesday   Full moon

31 Thursday   New Year's Eve

01 Friday   New Year's Day
Holiday, UK, Republic of Ireland, USA,
Canada, Australia and New Zealand

02 Saturday

03 Sunday

Tulipa maximowiczii, 1949

JANUARY

Holiday, Scotland and New Zealand

Monday 04

Tuesday 05

Last quarter
Epiphany

Wednesday 06

Thursday 07

Friday 08

Saturday 09

Sunday 10

Iris 'Thor', 1959

JANUARY

11 Monday

12 Tuesday

13 Wednesday   *New moon*

14 Thursday

15 Friday

16 Saturday

17 Sunday

Iris lortetii var. *samariae*, 1961

JANUARY

Holiday, USA (Martin Luther King Jnr Day) Monday 18

Tuesday 19

First quarter Wednesday 20

Thursday 21

Friday 22

Saturday 23

Sunday 24

Silene coronaria (syn. *Agrostemma coronaria*). Locality: Gorgan-Bojnurd; Iran, Altitude 5,000 ft., 1961

JANUARY

---

25 Monday

---

26 Tuesday   Holiday, Australia (Australia Day)

---

27 Wednesday

---

28 Thursday   *Full moon*

---

29 Friday

---

30 Saturday

---

31 Sunday

Anemone rivularis, 1959

FEBRUARY

Monday 01

Tuesday 02

Wednesday 03

Last quarter   Thursday 04

Friday 05

Accession of Queen Elizabeth II
Waitangi Day (New Zealand)   Saturday 06

Sunday 07

Bellevalia glauca. Locality: Northern Zagros, Iran, 1963

FEBRUARY

08 Monday   Holiday, New Zealand (Waitangi Day)

09 Tuesday

10 Wednesday

11 Thursday   *New moon*

12 Friday   Chinese New Year

13 Saturday

14 Sunday   Valentine's Day

Iris reticulata. This painting is one of a collection of paintings owned by the British Iris Society, c.1934

FEBRUARY

Holiday, USA (Presidents' Day)

Monday 15

Shrove Tuesday

Tuesday 16

Ash Wednesday

Wednesday 17

Thursday 18

First quarter

Friday 19

Saturday 20

Sunday 21

Cyclamen elegans. Locality: Hyrcanian Forest, Iran, 1965

FEBRUARY

22 Monday

23 Tuesday

24 Wednesday

25 Thursday

26 Friday

27 Saturday   Full moon

28 Sunday

Erythronium americanum, c.1963

MARCH

St David's Day

Monday 01

Tuesday 02

Wednesday 03

Thursday 04

Friday 05

Last quarter

Saturday 06

Sunday 07

Erythronium californicum 'White Beauty', c.1963

MARCH

08 *Monday*   Commonwealth Day

09 *Tuesday*

10 *Wednesday*

11 *Thursday*

12 *Friday*

13 *Saturday*   *New moon*

14 *Sunday*   Mothering Sunday,
UK and Republic of Ireland

Corydalis aitchisonii. P.F./6329. Locality: Badakhshan, Afghanistan, 1965

MARCH

Monday 15

Tuesday 16

St Patrick's Day
Holiday, Republic of Ireland
and Northern Ireland

Wednesday 17

Thursday 18

Friday 19

Vernal Equinox (Spring begins)

Saturday 20

First quarter

Sunday 21

Erythronium revolutum 'Rose Beauty', c.1950–65

MARCH

22 Monday

23 Tuesday

24 Wednesday

25 Thursday

26 Friday

27 Saturday

28 Sunday

Full moon
Palm Sunday
First day of Passover (Pesach)
British Summer Time begins

Iris 'Vulcanus' (*Regelio-cyclus* hybrid). This painting is one of a collection of paintings owned by the British Iris Society, 1959

MARCH/APRIL

Monday 29

Tuesday 30

Wednesday 31

Maundy Thursday

Thursday 01

Good Friday
Holiday, UK, Canada,
Australia and New Zealand

Friday 02

Saturday 03

Last quarter
Easter Sunday

Sunday 04

Allium mirum. P.F./5759. Locality: Northern spurs of Hindu Kush, above Jurm (East of Faizabad),
Afghanistan, 1965

APRIL

05 Monday

Easter Monday
Holiday, UK (exc. Scotland),
Republic of Ireland, Australia
and New Zealand

06 Tuesday

07 Wednesday

08 Thursday

09 Friday

10 Saturday

11 Sunday

Iris susiana, 1951

APRIL

New moon

Monday 12

First day of Ramadân
(subject to sighting of the moon)

Tuesday 13

Wednesday 14

Thursday 15

Friday 16

Saturday 17

Sunday 18

Allium noeanum. P.F./2000. Locality: South Kurdistan, Iraq, c.1965

APRIL

19 Monday

---

20 Tuesday — First quarter

---

21 Wednesday — Birthday of Queen Elizabeth II

---

22 Thursday

---

23 Friday — St George's Day

---

24 Saturday

---

25 Sunday — Anzac Day

Anemone blanda. i. Type. ii. *A. blanda* 'Ingramii' (syn. *A. blanda* 'Atrocoerulea'). iii. *A. blanda* 'Scythinica'. iv. *A. blanda* 'Alba'. v. *A. blanda* 'Rosea'. vi. Pale form. vii. Chance hybrid with *Anemone pavonina*, 1956

vi

v

vii

v

v

v

iii

iv

v

ii

ii

i

APRIL/MAY

Holiday, Australia and New Zealand
(Anzac Day)

Monday 26

Full moon

Tuesday 27

Wednesday 28

Thursday 29

Friday 30

Saturday 01

Sunday 02

Arum rupicola var. *rupicola* (syn. *Arum orientale* ssp. *engleri*). P.F./1893. Locality: 'Noa Kuh',
Khorramabad Gorge, Iran. Altitude: 6,000 ft., 1963

MAY

03 Monday

Last quarter
Early Spring Bank Holiday, UK
Holiday, Republic of Ireland

04 Tuesday

05 Wednesday

06 Thursday

07 Friday

08 Saturday

09 Sunday

Mother's Day, USA, Canada,
Australia and New Zealand

Fritillaria imperialis 'Aurora' (crown imperial 'Aurora'), undated

MAY

Monday 10

New moon

Tuesday 11

Wednesday 12

Ascension Day
Eid al-Fitr (end of Ramadân)
(subject to sighting of the moon)

Thursday 13

Friday 14

Saturday 15

Sunday 16

Anemone tschernjaewii. P.F./5643. Locality: Ghazni to Kabul, Afghanistan, 1965

MAY

17 *Monday*   Feast of Weeks (Shavuot)

18 *Tuesday*

19 *Wednesday*   *First quarter*

20 *Thursday*

21 *Friday*

22 *Saturday*

23 *Sunday*   Whit Sunday

Babiana stricta, 1959

MAY

Holiday, Canada (Victoria Day)

Monday 24

Tuesday 25

Full moon

Wednesday 26

Thursday 27

Friday 28

Saturday 29

Trinity Sunday

Sunday 30

Iris chrysographes forms. This painting is one of a collection of paintings now owned by the British Iris Society, 1949

MAY/JUNE

31 Monday

Spring Bank Holiday, UK
Holiday, USA (Memorial Day)

01 Tuesday

02 Wednesday

Last quarter
Coronation Day

03 Thursday

Corpus Christi

04 Friday

05 Saturday

06 Sunday

i. Crocus olivieri ii. Crocus nevadensis iii. Crocus veluchensis iv. Crocus angustifolius (syn. Crocus susianus minor), c.1965

Holiday, Republic of Ireland
Holiday, New Zealand (The Queen's Birthday)

Monday 07

Tuesday 08

Wednesday 09

New moon

Thursday 10

Friday 11

The Queen's Official Birthday
(subject to confirmation)

Saturday 12

Sunday 13

Crocosmia masoniorum. P.F. 8/61, August 1961

JUNE

---

14 Monday   Holiday, Australia (The Queen's Birthday)

---

15 Tuesday

---

16 Wednesday

---

17 Thursday

---

18 Friday   First quarter

---

19 Saturday

---

20 Sunday   Father's Day, UK, Republic of Ireland,
                                                                      USA and Canada

---

Erythronium dens-canis (syn. *Erythronium dens-canis roseum*), c.1963

JUNE

Summer solstice (Summer begins)

Monday 21

Tuesday 22

Wednesday 23

Full moon

Thursday 24

Friday 25

Saturday 26

Sunday 27

Anemone biflora. P.F./1495. Locality: Arak, Iran, 1962 Expedition notes: '*Anemone* sp. A glorious plant 2-3", all colours. 1-2" deep. Habitat: Growing with PF/1494 (Tulip), and generally pressed against the side and shade of a rock or large stone', 1963

JUNE/JULY

28 Monday

29 Tuesday

30 Wednesday

01 Thursday

Last quarter
Holiday, Canada (Canada Day)

02 Friday

03 Saturday

04 Sunday

Independence Day

Tulipa orphanidea subsp. *whittallii* (syn. *Tulipa whittallii*) and *Tulipa hageri*, 1951

JULY

Holiday, USA (Independence Day)

Monday 05

Tuesday 06

Wednesday 07

Thursday 08

Friday 09

New moon

Saturday 10

Sunday 11

Erythronium revolutum 'Pink Beauty', c.1963

JULY

12 Monday

Battle of the Boyne
Holiday, Northern Ireland

13 Tuesday

14 Wednesday

15 Thursday

St Swithin's Day

16 Friday

17 Saturday

First quarter

18 Sunday

Iris ensata (syn. *Iris kaemperi*), 1950

JULY

Monday 19

Tuesday 20

Wednesday 21

Thursday 22

Friday 23

Full moon   Saturday 24

Sunday 25

Amaryllis belladonna, 1948

JULY/AUGUST

26 Monday

27 Tuesday

28 Wednesday

29 Thursday

30 Friday

31 Saturday   *Last quarter*

01 Sunday

Anemone pavonina and Anemone hortensis (syn. Anemone stellata), 1956

AUGUST

Holiday, Scotland and Republic of Ireland

Monday 02

Tuesday 03

Wednesday 04

Thursday 05

Friday 06

Saturday 07

New moon

Sunday 08

Erythronium japonicum, c.1963

AUGUST

09 Monday

10 Tuesday   Islamic New Year

11 Wednesday

12 Thursday

13 Friday

14 Saturday

15 Sunday   First quarter

Arum rupicola (syn. *Arum conophalloides*) P.F./2298. Locality: 'Meshow Dagh', Azerbaijan, 1963

AUGUST

Monday 16

Tuesday 17

Wednesday 18

Thursday 19

Friday 20

Saturday 21

Full moon

Sunday 22

Bongardia chrysogonum. P.F./1197. Locality: Zagros mountain range, Iran, 1963

AUGUST

23 Monday

24 Tuesday

25 Wednesday

26 Thursday

27 Friday

28 Saturday

29 Sunday

Chlidanthus fragrans, 1957

AUGUST/SEPTEMBER

Last quarter
Summer Bank Holiday, UK
(exc. Scotland)

Monday 30

Tuesday 31

Wednesday 01

Thursday 02

Friday 03

Saturday 04

Father's Day, Australia
and New Zealand

Sunday 05

Iris vartanii var. *alba.* This painting is one of a collection of paintings now owned by the British
Iris Society, 1934

SEPTEMBER

06 *Monday*

Holiday, USA (Labor Day)
Holiday, Canada (Labour Day)

07 *Tuesday*

New moon
Jewish New Year (Rosh Hashanah)

08 *Wednesday*

09 *Thursday*

10 *Friday*

11 *Saturday*

12 *Sunday*

Fritillaria raddeana (syn. *Fritillaria askabadensis*), undated

SEPTEMBER

First quarter

Monday 13

Tuesday 14

Wednesday 15

Day of Atonement (Yom Kippur)

Thursday 16

Friday 17

Saturday 18

Sunday 19

Fritillaria meleagris pale forms. January 1961. Determinavit or reidentification by 'W.B.T'. (William Bertram Turrill), 1961

SEPTEMBER

---

20 Monday   *Full moon*

---

21 Tuesday   First day of Tabernacles (Succoth)

---

22 Wednesday   Autumnal Equinox (Autumn begins)

---

23 Thursday

---

24 Friday

---

25 Saturday

---

26 Sunday

Crocus banaticus (syn. *Crocus byzantinus* or *C. iridiflorus*), c.1965

SEPTEMBER/OCTOBER

Monday 27

Tuesday 28

Last quarter
Michaelmas Day

Wednesday 29

Thursday 30

Friday 01

Saturday 02

Sunday 03

Dierama pulcherrimum, 1957

OCTOBER

04 Monday

05 Tuesday

06 Wednesday   *New moon*

07 Thursday

08 Friday

09 Saturday

10 Sunday

Erythronium dens-canis Pale forms, c.1963

OCTOBER

Holiday, USA (Columbus Day)
Holiday, Canada (Thanksgiving)

Monday 11

Tuesday 12

First quarter

Wednesday 13

Thursday 14

Friday 15

Saturday 16

Sunday 17

Erythronium revolutum Johnsonii Group, c.1963

OCTOBER

18 Monday

19 Tuesday

20 Wednesday   *Full moon*

21 Thursday

22 Friday

23 Saturday

24 Sunday

Fritillaria raddeana. P.F./5128 Locality: 'Transcapian Iran', Caspian or Northern Iran,
Golestan Forest. 1965

OCTOBER

Holiday, Republic of Ireland
Holiday, New Zealand (Labour Day)

Monday 25

Tuesday 26

Wednesday 27

Last quarter

Thursday 28

Friday 29

Saturday 30

Halloween
British Summer Time ends

Sunday 31

Fritillaria hispanica. Determinavit or reidentification by 'W.B.T.' (William Bertram Turrill), 1961

NOVEMBER

01 *Monday*   All Saints' Day

02 *Tuesday*

03 *Wednesday*

04 *Thursday*   *New moon*

05 *Friday*   Guy Fawkes

06 *Saturday*

07 *Sunday*

Tulipa mauritiana. 'Neo T' (neo- tulip), 1951

NOVEMBER

Monday 08

Tuesday 09

Wednesday 10

First quarter
Holiday, USA (Veterans Day)
Holiday, Canada (Remembrance Day)

Thursday 11

Friday 12

Saturday 13

Remembrance Sunday

Sunday 14

Iris acutiloba subsp. *lineolata* (syn. *Iris helenae*) PF. 6/61. This painting is one of a collection of paintings now owned by the British Iris Society, 1961

NOVEMBER

15 *Monday*

16 *Tuesday*

17 *Wednesday*

18 *Thursday*

19 *Friday*   *Full moon*

20 *Saturday*

21 *Sunday*

Fritillaria imperialis, undated

NOVEMBER

Monday 22

Tuesday 23

Wednesday 24

Holiday, USA (Thanksgiving)

Thursday 25

Friday 26

Last quarter

Saturday 27

First Sunday in Advent
Hannukah begins (at sunset)

Sunday 28

Lilium bakerianum var. *delavayi* (syn. *Lilium delavayi*). 'Painted from sketches made in 1948, when the lilies flowered with Mr. Constable who received them from Dr. Rock', 1955

29 Monday

30 Tuesday   St Andrew's Day

01 Wednesday

02 Thursday

03 Friday

04 Saturday   New moon

05 Sunday

Bellevalia lipskyi. P.F./1745. Locality: 'Kuh i Dareh-Bid', North Zagros, Iran, 1963

DECEMBER

Hannukah ends

Monday 06

Tuesday 07

Wednesday 08

Thursday 09

Friday 10

First quarter

Saturday 11

Sunday 12

Iris unguicularis var. Collected in Crete, undated

DECEMBER

13 *Monday*

14 *Tuesday*

15 *Wednesday*

16 *Thursday*

17 *Friday*

18 *Saturday*

19 *Sunday*

Full moon

Colchicum hirsutum (but many-flowered). Locality: Kazerun to Shiraz, 30 degrees West of Shiraz, Iran, Altitude 6,500 ft. 1963

DECEMBER

Monday 20

Winter Solstice (Winter begins)   Tuesday 21

Wednesday 22

Thursday 23

Christmas Eve   Friday 24

Christmas Day   Saturday 25

Boxing Day (St Stephen's Day)   Sunday 26

Fritillaria latifolia (syn. *Fritillaria lutea* var. *latifolia*). Determinavit or reidentification by 'W.B.T.'
(William Bertram Turrill), c.1961

27 *Monday*

Last quarter
Holiday, UK, Republic of Ireland,
USA, Canada, Australia and
New Zealand (Christmas Day)

28 *Tuesday*

Holiday, UK, Republic of Ireland,
USA, Canada, Australia
and New Zealand (Boxing Day)

29 *Wednesday*

30 *Thursday*

31 *Friday*

New Year's Eve

01 *Saturday*

New Year's Day

02 *Sunday*

Anemone biflora, 1963

YEAR PLANNER

JANUARY	JULY
FEBRUARY	AUGUST
MARCH	SEPTEMBER
APRIL	OCTOBER
MAY	NOVEMBER
JUNE	DECEMBER